THE
FARMER
GIVES
THANKS

THE
FARMER
GIVES
THANKS

SAMUEL R. GUARD

ABINGDON PRESS
New York Nashville

THE FARMER GIVES THANKS

Library of Congress Catalog Card Number: 56-10145

SET UP, PRINTED, AND BOUND BY THE
PARTHENON PRESS, AT NASHVILLE,
TENNESSEE, UNITED STATES OF AMERICA

TO

THE HUSBANDMAN
That Laboureth

"The husbandman that laboureth must be first partaker of the fruits."

—II TIM. 2:6

These words are graven in stone above the great bronze doors of the house of the United States Department of Agriculture in Washington, D.C.

PREFACE

THE FARMER is a poet, and don't you forget it! Of course he would be the first to spit in the dust and deny it if you accused him of doffing his hat as the sun comes rolling red gold and bright silver up out of the hill pasture; of stopping the mower for a full hour to whittle a splint for a meadow lark's broken wing; of clucking in glee as he lays off a new land and glimpses how straight and smooth and black is that furrow.

The farmer is an artist too. Incomparable. Except that his clay is living red muscle; his "lost-wax," fat; his colors, chromosomes; his brushes, currycombs; his exhibit, a blue-ribbon pumpkin or a champion Shorthorn that weighs a half-ton in a year.

The farmer is a believer. Naturally a believer. He plows in faith; he sows in hope; he reaps in charity. From morning milking to midnight farrow the farmer witnesses personally: "All things come of thee, O Lord, and of thine own have we given thee."

God brought every beast of the field to the first farmer to see what he would call them. And blessing the farmer and his helpmeet, the Lord God gave them dominion over every herb, every tree yielding seed, and over every thing that moved upon the earth. That dominion is still the farmer's duty, and his discipline too. It makes him, here on earth, a working partner with his Father in heaven. Instinctively the farmer believes; naturally he worships; and gentleman that he is—with plants and animals, and children—he gives thanks, silently, or in slow, earnest words, to his gracious Landlord in the sky.

How do I know? With my own eyes I have seen an old farmer at the supper table, surrounded by his children and grandchildren, his wife there at yon end between the hired man and the high chair, and with my own ears I have listened to his grace. All you have to do to write a book like this is to listen.

Of course the farmer is interested in the price of his hogs, in feeding supplement to his cattle, in the tariff on wool, in parity prices—but there's something deeper. What's he really thinking? As he prays in his heart, what does he say? The first of these prayers opened "Sam Guard's Roundup" in the October, 1947, issue of *Breeder's Gazette*. Every issue of my farm paper since then has opened with prayer. Subscribers have requested prayers to recite in Sunday school, at the woman's club, the 4-H Congress. Some church papers have reprinted them. And now Abingdon Press has put them into a little book.

O I thank thee, Author of all. For thine is the power, and the glory. Amen.

Samuel R. Guard

In the gray night's end, O Lord, we watched thee like a careful sheep herder drive the Pleiades out of our farm's sky just in time to make room for the sun, wheeling into our east meadow to defrost the rye grass for the ewes.

Thank thee, Lord.

Help us indeed to welcome the new year with happy hearts, even as we welcomed that newborn calf.

Bless every bird and beast in the barn.

Bless every child which thou has so confidently housed here.

May we walk every furrow uprightly all the new year through; and what we do harvest, may we share it gladly, unafraid.

Thank thee for the old year, Lord, every thing, every day —from the whinny of the chestnut mare in the morning to the welcoming bark of old Shep at sundown.

And help us not to mind any longer the briars across the far end of yon pathway.

Are they not rose briars after all?

Look, Lord, these two horny hands that we thought were clasped, are cups now: this one to recive and this one to pass on thy measureless bounty every day.

AMEN

9

The cock crows.

Snow crunches underfoot.

The east pasture rises reddish, gold, silver, out of the dark.

Briskly we unlatch the barnyard gate and let the new year in.

Happy New Year it is.

Anno Domini.

Year of our Lord!

O, we thank thee, great God above, eternal Keeper of time, Dispatcher of the years.

We thank thee for the year that has closed, and for the year that has come.

Nature rests; we plan.

We planned back there to leave the sheep and carry an ephah of parched grain to our brothers on yon mountainside, where the brash giant then defied the armies of the living God.

And thou didst help us, O Lord of hosts, to choose five smooth stones out of the brook.

O, we thank thee.

But keep us humble.

AMEN

Almighty Timekeeper, eternal God, which art from ever-lasting to everlasting, whose mighty power of love and cohesion transcends the explosive terror of all the atoms in the universe, we pray as little children pray, in utter trust and devotion.

Our Father, we would enter the glistening gates of the year with sunlit wonder in our eyes and dewy gladness in our hearts.

Make us strong to clear pathways and kill weeds, but gentle to yean lambs and tend cattle, for whose meat and milk, and wool, we thank thee much.

Mostly, make us patient, Lord, all through the year, that we may love our neighbor as ourselves, and thee beyond all.

AMEN

Humble and uncovered, our Father, we bow again inside the gateway of time.

We could not see very far down New Year's Lane, O Lord, so confused and tangled and tortuous it seems in there.

Help us to trim up all those dead brambles and fill the chuckholes of doubt with rocks of our granite faith.

Help us to make the way straight, as the Baptist cried in the other wilderness by Jordan.

And may we bank the road with greensward and flowers and quiet little shrines to thy everlasting mercy.

For Epiphany, every Sunday we praise thee; and for Plough Monday too, when we rededicate our toil to the feeding of thy lambs the world around.

Till the chief Shepherd shall appear.

Amen

Snowdrifts! Scudding clouds! The harsh wind!

But we mind them not, dear Lord.

Snow will have filled the stock pond.

Clouds will have fooled the ground hog.

Harsh wind will have planted flower seeds in the fence row.

Help us, our Father, in twenty and eight days to do the work of thirty-one, and to catch up on our reading too.

O Great Shepherd, bless the dumb creatures hereabouts as they multiply, that we may have more meat for our strength—we who go striding out, so well-booted and so well-bundled from their substance, to encounter the gale and laugh at the storm.

For health and plenty and hickory wood, we thank thee.

With humble hearts.

But big plans!

Amen

For battened barn and heated home, for oaten straw and hickory wood, for silage sweet and turnip greens, for soybean meal and fowl fit to eat, we do thank thee, Great Provider.

Though the days be short, our evenings are long.

Though the month be short, our plans are long.

Only three phases of the snow moon, but there's no blood upon it now, thanks be to God.

That both peace and plenty do come from thee, we lisp like children, glad and grateful.

Bless then this meat to our use, our selves to thy service, here and beyond, now and forever.

Amen

Our Father, who let there be lights for signs, and for seasons, we thank thee for the ice that plows our sodden soil; for the snow that waters our buttercups, sleeping; for the frost that etches our windows with stars; for the baritone breeze that quickens our chores.

And we thank thee, God, for this bread and meat which give us warm red blood enough to meet the cold challenge of these times, and in all good hope.

Who harnessed the storm and gave us the lightning to read by? Who dressed our lambs in wool, our calves in curls, and our pigs in sense enough to huddle together?

Thee, blessed Lord, our holy Landlord.

O we thank thee!

And that the wind is in the south!

AMEN

Herder of the stars in the sky, we are grateful for the short month.

For unlatching the heavens and letting the new moon out. This snow must melt and this ice will gurgle into our stock pond under thy strengthening sunshine.

Even so, all our cold tears must turn to sweetwater under the warmth of thy everlasting care and sprout the seeds of hope stored high and dry in our hearts.

Put thine unerring finger on our compass, Lord, that we run this terrace rightly and plan a year's work on this farm that will delight our Great Landlord.

Whether we seed, weed, feed, or breed, walk close by and lend us the counsel of the Good Shepherd, all of whose lambs we will feed, even as thou feedest us.

AMEN

Dear Lord and Partner, we never saw the snow so deep on the pathway to the barn, but we know that's mighty good for the pasture and the plowed oats ground.

Lord, was that funny green patch snowdrops, crocuses, or just clover, that we uncovered there by the lilac bushes?

We've got so much to eat here, dear Lord, we're going to put half this ham aside for some kids in need.

We would thank thee, Keeper of the record books, for an old farmer named George Washington who laid out this nation, and for the Rail Splitter, too, who never would hear to any new line-fence smack through the center, but kept it all together for us.

Make us good husbandlike tenants ever, and worthy of thy bounty.

AMEN

Our Father, comes February and we recall that from the rude hut where Abraham Lincoln was born to the mansarded mansion where George Washington came into the world is a good ten days' journey, by calendar or horseback.

All along the way, in miles or months, thou didst abundantly bless us, extending our lands to the seven seas and our meekness to inherit the earth.

We thank thee, our Saviour, that we can now give of this meat and drink, take in the stranger, clothe the naked, visit the sick and in prison, and minister to them.

Bless our new captains, O Lord of hosts; bless our captains over tens, over fifties, over hundreds, and over thousands.

Amen

Who shall rebuke the winds of March or calm the raging snow waters?

Who but thee, O Lord, who slept in the hinder part of the ship and commanded us to be not fearful.

And told the storm: be still.

Give us that same great faith, O God, as we come into the new spring.

Bless our plows, and our harrows too.

Let our grass seed fall on good ground, rot naturally in the moist earth, and live again in the warmth of the sun.

Bless every suckling thing on this place, our Father.

Strengthen the mothers, and spread their tender spirit of love and sacrifice into the hearts of men the world around.

We saw the wild geese in echelon flying, O God, and we are thankful.

Amen

Father above, the sun swept away the hoarfrost and there was a crocus, blooming his heart out—a chalice of gold!

We peeked in the barn door, and there she was, up again, twin lambs at her side!

Help us to see that out of pain comes forth peace; out of storm, calm; out of fierce thunderheads, the blessed rains; out of a rent loin, honey.

If thou dost measure these winds to the sheep that are shorn, what have we to fear?

May new grass flourish the earth around.

May all the babes have milk enough.

And may we have sense enough to apportion plentitude, in thy name, who givest all.

Amen

For lively new creatures with pink noses that this old farmer helped into a glistering but beautiful world last night, we thank thee, Lord.

Thy children are fussing again, our Father, and we who are left on this patch of black earth here are in sore need of bright courage and stout faith.

Strengthen us for any struggle, Lord.

Temper this wind to the lamb that is shorn.

If the crocus bloom, can Johnny-jump-up be far behind?

Make us patient, but well-prepared.

AMEN

Father in the wind-blown heavens, we watch in wonderment as you set plumb again the axle of our greening earth.

Even at the sixth hour this morning we needed no lantern to attend those blessed yeaning things on the bright rye straw in the big red barn.

Now when the daytime gets as long as the night,
God's new springtime is here surely enough.

Make us as ready as the robins are.

For whenever the time may come, we want to turn over to you more than five barley loaves and two little fishes.

Make us strong but humble; just, but kind; and every day, rain or shine, smiling.

AMEN

For longer days and lesser nights we were glad, O Lord, our God, who tilteth this burgeoning earth in the hollow of thine almighty hand so that the vernal sun can rise straight out of the east and set plumb in our west pasture —an ordered world.

We need that extra time to rake and disk and plow and plant so that thy good creatures may all be fed.

Help us, Lord, to run clean furrows, straight or rightly curved to the contour.

For all these calves and lambs and pigs and fluffy chicks, we give thee praise.

Make us gentle with all of them, but just, too, so that we may tender the meat of strength and the milk of kindness to all the children of thine image the globe about.

And give us peace, within, without, forever.

AMEN

Lent is sacrifice, but Lent is spring.

So we do thank thee, Father in heaven, for reining the sun up this way again; for making these warming days as long as the starry nights with the growing moon.

Would our Lord have need for our colt today?

Before the very stones cry out, we wave branches and shout, "Hosanna; Blessed is he that cometh in the name of the Lord."

But must our righteous King be crucified?

Must our viable seed be buried in the dark earth?

Thy will be done.

AMEN

Hosanna, hosanna in the highest!

Our moon fills; our grass greens; our daffodils bloom; our catbird trills. The calving was easy; twin lambs nurse; and thirteen new pigs!

The clover roots sing as they leap from the moldboard, and we who drive—healthy, strong, and eager—would wave branches too.

When suddenly, is darkness at noon; a dying One is given vinegar for drink; the veil of the temple is rent in twain from the top to the bottom.

Eli, Eli, lama sabachthani?

A big stone locks the grave.

Tearful, sweat-faced, we dig soil with what faith we have left; we bury seed in hope.

For thy children must be fed.

But behold! The stone is rolled away! The seed is quickened! The Lord is risen!

Thanks be to thee, O God, our Father eternal.

AMEN

O risen Lord, Father, Comforter, we send up our thanks for these towheads bowed; for their stout little hands that help us harrow the fields and broadcast the seeds, hay the steers and milk the cows.

But if in their sweet whispers they should open every job with prayer, if the sons and daughters of their daughters and sons, yonder, add their thanks to ours—'t were not enough to drain our heartsprings of their never-failing flow of praise to thee, our Father.

For thine everlasting mercy to us; for sending the shining angel to roll away the stone and to say: "Fear not ye. . . . for he is risen."

Our dogwoods now wave a cross from every blossom and surround that blushing Judas tree, even as our grass seeds burst their cerements and the brown bulk, buried, rises into a glorious Easter lily, gently nodding in the breath from heaven.

O we do thank thee for all, Father of all.

AMEN

Almighty Creator, who gathered the waters together unto one place and let this dry land appear, we thank thee that we could plow a furrow clean.

And now with our horse of iron, two, three, and even four furrows, at one round!

Even as thy Son taught us, help us to sow our seed on good ground; not by the wayside, upon stony places, nor among thorns.

Make us like the Good Shepherd to know our sheep and be known of them.

Bless every calf, pig, colt, chick, and child on this place, O Lord.

We are so glad that we could set the rooftree and tie the rafters to the beams.

We thank thee, O God, specially for the gentle rains.

But no storm, on land or sea or in the governments of men, is harsh enough to cast down our hearts after you set your rainbow in the sky.

And arrayed these Easter lilies.

O grave, where is thy victory?

The Lord is risen!

Praise God.

AMEN

God, who set thy bow in the cloud, we thank thee for this token of the covenant between us.

We thank thee, too, for the chance to tend again our own bright patch of greening ground.

The grass springs, the flowers bloom, the birds sing, our calves frolic—this whole farm acts like a gaily arrayed chorus of praise to thee.

Having watched a shriveled brown bulb burst its black burial place and rise as a lily, white and gilded for the Easter altar, who can doubt the resurrecting power of thy boundless love, our Father?

AMEN

Bright little crocuses scampered clear across the dooryard to tell the forsythia bush; dewy daffodils nodded all day to the sugar maple tree; the red buds wouldn't wait for their new garments of green—nor we, to thank thee for the spring.

The lambs jump higher than the old ewe's back; the pink-nosed pigs nudge for dear life; the calves take to the creek as the ducklings to the pond; while we thy children in thine own image claim anew the covenant of thy bow in the cloud.

Preserve us from flood of war as thou didst Noah from the waters of the flood.

Help us to plow deep, harrow fine, and to seed as if every seed were to bear bread to be broken by the Lord himself.

Amen

We thank thee, Lord, for the clubs of thy children come unto this country temple on rural church day—Sabbath of the Rogation.

As that other flock-keeper turned aside to see the burning bush, so come we in wonderment to this holy ground, listening to the call of God.

Thanks be to thee for a seedbed that is warm.

Thanks for the clover with four leaves.

Thanks for the brooder that glows gently and the shears that sing.

Our thinking heads, our loyal hearts, our serving hands, our living health we would dedicate to the Lord's work—in country and town, the world around.

In the shadow of thy wing keep all our old members, carrying cross or hoe or gun.

Leader supreme, lend thy helping hand to our project every day, and help us to complete it as thy good and faithful servants.

AMEN

If that gnarled old pear tree in the hog lot can tend such a grand bouquet of blossoms, surely we can offer a garland of kind deeds to man and beast ever to please thee, our Lord.

As the slim crescent in our night sky grows into the bright full moon, most favorable for maize planting, may we round out our lives with the fullness of God, as the tentmaker said.

Waft our seed onto good earth, O Lord, and let it bear a hundredfold—feed for thy creatures and meat for thy children the world around.

AMEN

That we have meat and can eat, we thank thee, God.

And, O blessed Landlord, we who are let to work this bit of holy earth, do pray thee to walk beside us as we sow.

Watch over us, our Father, to be good tenants, and worthy of this partnership which we seal with our toil.

We thank thee, Lord, for all these flowers; all this green stuff for the silo too.

Bless the shearing, Good Shepherd; and as we tie the fleece, strain the milk, and replenish the self-feeder, help us to remember the least of these, thy brethren.

AMEN

Our Father in high heaven, omnipotent to part the dark clouds and stretch the seven-colored string of yon bright rainbow from rising stock pond to harrowed maize field, we do thank thee for these showers.

But we've plowed deep down, even sub-soiled, in full faith that thy mercy endureth.

Like the fragrance from these lilacs, our rogation rises to thee that our flocks multiply, our crops yield even a hundredfold, that we may feed thy lambs, thy sheep.

Good Shepherd, forgive our straying, and protect us, we implore thee, Redeemer divine.

AMEN

Lord, God, the same who walked in Adam's garden in the cool of the day, we thank thee now for all these flowers.

Especially for the flowers with honey in them.

We thank thee for a month with two full moons, and a barn with four "Very Good" cows that give milk three times a day now—so green are thy pastures.

Make us no less gay than bobolink as he moves into that thorn-apple bush so grandly whitewashed by thy mysterious hand.

Count every click of our planter a prayer to thee to bless the seed.

Bless every chick and calf, every shote and sheep, every cat and canary bird hereabouts.

Bless every child; with wisdom and stature endow them; and number us, too, among thy children forevermore.

AMEN

We bow our heads; we open our hearts.

Who painted the rainbow in the sky?

Who greened the grass, arrayed the lily?

Who fed our mockingbird through the winter and sent him back again all that way to sing atop the cupola on our barn?

Who put the gambol in those lambs, and the merry smile on baby's face?

Who broke the brown cerements of the seed with a frond so tender you never could imagine how it ever got out?

Who made a little farmer feel as strong as an ox,

Yet as gentle as a ewe with twins?

Who baled this family together with bonds of love and work and beauty?

Our Lord.

Our risen Lord!

O we thank thee!

Amen

Almighty Keeper of the seasons, whose hand but thine could have banked the earth so skillfully or again ridden the sun from Capricorn to Cancer without a bobble, bringing us so glorious a summer?

This grass and hay, we would graze with better beasts and harvest with willing hands, so that all thy children might have milk and meat.

Help us, O Lord, to blast the pests and the weeds as the devil and his plagues.

Bless the brides.

The graduates too.

Thanks be to thee for decorating the world with all these roses.

For them, and for us.

AMEN

Master, we do see the fig tree and all the trees; they do now shoot forth, and we know of our own selves that summer is now at hand, as you told them in the meetings at the Mount of Olives.

O Lord, we planted in full farmer-faith when the oak leaf was as big as a mouse's ear, and behold the contoured corn has four blades already.

The longest day of the year is yet not long enough to delimit our praise for thy constant goodness to us, O God.

Make us worthy and kind, and just, and pure like those white roses from Mother's garden.

AMEN

God, who in the beginning said, "Let the earth bring forth grass, . . . and it was so," we that pasture the cattle and fold the sheep come from the hayfield to thank thee for thy ever-loving kindness, thy never-ending mercy.

Didst not thou tilt the axis of this green earth toward thy great heart that we might have lengthening days, and warmer?

Creator almighty—who put life in mud, greensward in hayseed, increase in sows, song in catbirds, roses in thorns, and brotherly love even in the hearts of us—bless this food to our use and our lives to thy service.

Thy service now, on this farm, the world around, and forevermore.

AMEN

Eternal God, in whose image are we, our summer-song is psalm to thee—for all these green pastures.

Receive, O Father above, the fragrance of this first cutting as incense of our farmer-love rising to heaven from our little altar of earth down here.

Watching the clover join forces with our June grass, trading nitrogen for humus, and both thriving the more, we can see how one gets by giving.

From early sunup to late sundown we gladly work to make more meat and strip more milk that all thy children may be fed to new strength in thy service, whether in field or shop, mine or ship, pulpit or potato patch.

Send rain to the parched plains, Lord.

AMEN

H'm-m-m, the incense of new-mown hay burning in the sun!

H'm-m-m, the smell of rambler roses climbing our barn-yard fence.

Thy footstool is upholstered in new green, O Lord, bound 'round with old gold.

As the long days come, we thank thee, O God, for all this infinite alchemy of nature that lets us farmer folk transmute ashes into attar, and mud into meat.

Make us not ashamed, our Father, to replant where the water stood, or the locusts devoured, or we just plain missed in our hurry to make the turn before you wheeled the sun about toward Capricorn.

Give us peace within and without, O God, and thine be the glory forevermore.

AMEN

As the very sun stood still in the sky at summer's solstice, so pause we at this turnrow in heartful thanks to thee for the green glory of thy teeming earth, O God.

Bless this whole country.

Strengthen this nation.

Silence the selfish.

Sustain the liberators.

And in thine everlasting arms encircle them with safety and us with hope.

AMEN

Our Father, a million blades in our cornfield gaily wave their green banners to thee in very joy of growing.

So we raise our arms to thee in praise for lives planted with roots in good earth.

Strengthen our brace roots against any wind or flood.

We thank thee, our Creator, that thou didst endow us with certain unalienable rights; that among these are Life, Liberty and the Pursuit of Happiness.

O make us worthy, and make our sons as brave as thy Son and as ready to hand vengeance back to thee.

You repay, Lord, and give us peace now and forevermore.

Amen

Our Father, God, that we have bread to break, strength to work, ease to take, we thank thee, Giver of all.

We cut bitter weed, but gather altar flowers for thee, Landlord eternal.

We celebrate now that thou didst let us split the atom and harness the sun.

But make us meek enough about it to inherit the earth.

May the sharp crackle of our myriad maize plants through these hot nights herald the march of liberty around the world.

"For thine is the kingdom, and the power, and the glory, for ever."

Amen

Captain of the eternal guard, on these acres of black drill ground we are all present or accounted for.

Those caissons which go rolling along up and down the corn rows are panoplied with plows and not with powder.

We put up hay, make grass silage, seed sweet sudan, that every one in thy image may have milk and meat enough.

So for these heavy lambs, healthful heifers, pink-combed pullets, and pigs well weaned we would give thee our farmer thanks.

Make us just as glad to share our blessings as to glory in our work.

And on this day we pray again for independence under God, for every person and for every people in this world.

AMEN

Gracious Landlord in the skies, we are so glad you renewed our lease.

May we ever be partners.

God of the prophet, God of the herdsman, we thank thee for sending the rain on the new pasture, and just right on our hayfield.

With trumpet of truth we sound our independence of tyrants, but our dependence of thee.

Whether with broken bell or supersonic escadrille, we will proclaim liberty throughout all the land unto all the inhabitants thereof.

And on the morrow take the butter-brightness of another full moon as a sign of thy favor.

We thank thee, too, Giver of every good and perfect gift, for lambs marketed and corn laid by.

AMEN

Lord God of hosts, may he never have to go again to war, leaving his plow in that fall furrow.

Must old men once more put the sword handle back on the pruning hook?

Is this good red meat to build our strength for war instead of peace?

We thank thee for the heat that makes our corn to grow.

And all these blackberries.

We thank thee for the breeze, too, the maple shade and the ponds full of rain water.

Give us of wisdom enough to decide what's right, of blood red enough to face the truth, and of courage enough thy will to do.

AMEN

For putting the dog days on the leash, we would give thee praise, our Father.

We farmers come now to the day of reckoning.

We can see where we plowed deep and where we cut corners.

Reverently we celebrate the loaf-mass of our forefathers and we place on thine altar the first fruits of our harvest; if needs be we will bring more to feed all thy lambs.

And now bless us as we show the firstlings of our flocks and herds for ribbons of white and yellow and red and blue.

Help us like real men to be glad with what we get; and to accept the adjudgment in humble assurance that with thy continued help we can do even better in producing the meats and the milk, the bread and the butter, the cool fiber, and the warm, whereby little children flourish and the elder ones are comforted.

Behold, O Lord, if the harvest truly is great, may we labor among the other seventy also.

AMEN

Mighty Showman of the skies, who hast lined up the stars with the planets and commanded the moon and the sun to attend in our vast water-colored arena festooned with clouds, make our farmer-judgment ever sound and good and right.

These first fruits are thine, O Lord, and the flower of our flocks.

We bring them with thankful hearts, for our neighbors who have none, and even for those of whom it hath been said, "An eye for an eye," and a "tooth for a tooth."

And as we exchange our food and fiber for raiment and roof, may the trade be fair and altogether pleasing to thee, our God and our Redeemer.

AMEN

Beloved Foreman, who in the beginning worked for six days and rested on the seventh and saw that the job was very good, help us likewise to honor sweat, exalt skill, and dignify labor.

Above all, we pray that we may do honest work for a fair wage as free men 'round the globe—whether on range or steppes, in cornfield or rice paddy, at forge or desk, farm or factory, tank or tractor, with pruning hook or sword.

If defend we must, we would fight from heaven and labor for thee.

Lord God of harvests, we thank thee that the full moon yet will ride again so serenely after a total eclipse over our still-prolific fields.

For this fruitful fall and ripening frost we are glad.

Strengthen us to the harvest, and make this laborer worthy of his hire.

AMEN

Father, which art in heaven, our green banners turn to brown of ripening—and then to gold of harvest.

And we turn to thee in praise.

Our daily bread is here, and in such plenty that we would share with all thy children.

Now that we have sundered the infinitesimal, and crowd ever closer the secrets of life and death, we need thee more and more.

So tremendous is this power, newly placed by thee in our hands, but old in the sun, that we must be kind and just and walk humbly with our God.

We would harness the atom for peace and not for war, and we ask thy special blessing on all who say so.

AMEN

Wonderful Counsellor, the mighty God, the everlasting Father, the Prince of peace: O we thank thee.

Sojourn done.

School begun.

Of him who fell among thieves we shall not pass by on the other side, but we will bind up his wounds and, with thy help, take care of him.

For meat to eat, we thank thee.

For tasseled corn and purple grapes, for bluegrass green again and pullets laying, for mellow hides and silken hair, for our proper place in the great parade of livestock and of life, we praise thee.

Beloved Ringmaster, planets and protons alike march in array at thy gentle command.

May we, thy children, walk humbly, our hand in thine, do justly, love mercy evermore, our Father.

AMEN

Almighty God, who holdest the yellow moon like a cherry bowl on the tips of thy fingers, is not our newly cleaned and covered corncrib an altar to thee?

As the silk retreats into the browning shuck, as the sap recedes and the day grows shorter, as the dahlias dance and the fringed gentians put on blue veils, as the apple seed darkens and the milkweed blows fairy cotton all over the place, as the blackbirds hold county convention and the patriarch swallow calls his family together, as the ewe weans her lambs and the calves let their hair grow, we know, Good Landlord, that another Harvest Home is come.

We thank thee for all this plenty that we are now to ingather.

And we pray thee for peace.

For enduring peace, based on this plenty, around the world.

AMEN

For the bright fall flowers on this table, we praise thee, Lord, and for the pumpkin of gold and the squash with the crooked neck.

This whole centerpiece is a little altar where we bow our heads to our gracious God, who feeds us so bountifully, even of meat and milk.

We thank thee for another September that opened with a paean to Labor and closes with a hymn to Atonement; and for a full moon that is a harvest moon.

Make us glad when fall begins and accountable when the night is as long as the day.

We who had rain will share with the just ones who had little.

Give us Elijah's faith, O Lord God.

Was that not a little cloud like a man's hand that we saw arising the seventh time we went up?

Green our pastures once again before frost for the benefit of our four-footed friends, and thine, over whom thou hast given us dominion.

Make us worthy tenants of thy kingdom now and evermore, O God.

AMEN

Almighty Harvest Hand, let us work alongside thee.

Help us glean.

And stack.

And soundly store.

God, who turns the green to gold, the milky dough into a kernel of feed, the bawling calf into a gentle cow lowing with tenderness, turn thou this bounteous fall festival into an ingathering of food for banquet and for succor.

Yet a little longer keep the hoarfrost haltered.

We are so grateful, Lord of the harvest, for the wheel of the locust grinding melancholy into gladness, for the come-lately zinnia blooming like flame, for bluegrass lush again with the white clover 'mongst it, for hickory sticks on the old dog irons.

Bring safely back those who warmed their little hands here; and bless them, gird them, uphold them, whatever their missions, or how many they be.

AMEN

Put it in our horny hands as it is in our farmer hearts,
O Lord, to be careful—very careful—with this harvest.

Our hay's in mow, oats in bin, silage in trench.

But 'tis not so with all thy folk, we do remember.

The white sow farrowed ten again and saved them all.

The rye springs green and the husks turn gold.

The picker stands greased; two rows at a time!

The pullets cluck a new tune. The calves are weaned and
the milk cans heavier.

School keeps.

The frost bites a little, but opens the hulls.

Our sheet-iron rooster heads northward, mostly.

A hunter's moon fills with refulgent light and our souls
fill with gladness.

Thanks be to thee, O gracious Giver, God.

AMEN

For white meat to eat, and wool to wear, for rooftree strong, farm work to share, we give thee thanks, O blessed Lord.

For the gold in our cribs and the sleek on our cattle, we thank thee too.

Guide our hand on election day.

Endow our chosen leaders with wisdom, honor, and strength.

May the plenty of our farmstuffs, shared, plant good will in the hearts of men the world around.

That the harvest may be peace and we may be called the children of God, forever.

Amen

Lord of the harvest, what was that you said, witnessing the scattered sheep without a shepherd on the browning Judean hills?

Oh, yes: "The harvest truly is plenteous, but the labourers are few."

Didst mean us here on this old stock farm?

But we are very thankful for tractors that purr, for pickers that steadily shuck our hybrid ears, for elevators that cure backaches, and for all the motors that sing as they work and light us on our way.

Make us worthy of a plenteous harvest.

Help us to get it all and to use it so that every one in thy image may be fed to grow in strength and grace.

Specially shepherd thy sheep scattered abroad, O Lord, and temper the wind where they're shorn.

AMEN

Son of man, we do give humble thanks to our Father, God, that we have a place where to lay our heads, raiment of sheep's wool, and bread with butter on it.

If we did have to sell our gobblers, we can still thank thee for a good fat hen, garnished in tart red berries from the vanishing bog.

If the frost bit our garden, it did ripen the corn,

the golden corn from which our lovely critters will extract milk for the children and meat for their mothers.

If our Pilgrim forefathers could set foot on a rock, fell stout timbers for rooftrees, and grind calico maize into meal, surely we can adjust our lives to new frontiers of peace and plenty.

With thy help we will, God of our fathers, as we praise thy holy name forever.

AMEN

L ord of harvests, Keeper of our feedlots and our fields, we thank thee for a turkey that is fat.

We thank thee for bread with butter on it.

We wish we could echo in these poor words the glorious autumn song of praise that rises from our frosted, browning stalks of corn, bent with ears of gold.

Accept the fragrance of red clover in yon mow as burnt incense rising from the holy earthen altar of this here stock farm.

Help us to be humble, just, and kind as thy servant said—specially kind to those creatures over whom thou gave us original dominion, which we have subdued and fattened and multiplied and milked according to thy direction.

Make us good shepherds to them as thou art the Good Shepherd to us.

Bless all thine own children about this board, or absent from it.

And make our hearts big enough to receive thy bounty in constant thanksgiving.

AMEN

Our Father, of hallowed name, as we journey up in spirit with that other family to be enrolled, we praise thee for today.

O look ye down from heaven high to this steaming board —decked now with red apples from our orchard and green cedars from our graveyard, laden with meat from our flock and milk from our kine, bread from our stubble and sweetenin' from our maples—and bless our table as a holy altar of thank offering.

From the gracious lady at yon end to your old farmer right here, from stalwart son to lovely daughter, from gurgling baby to our good old hired hand, from kin to kith the world around—we all, dear God, like those other shepherds, would heed the heavenly host.

AMEN

Our Father, who art in heaven—as the short days come, we would be humble.

As the long nights chill, we would be kind.

As the old year wanes, we would be just.

We thank thee, Lord, for harvest garnered, for brood cows sheltered, for holly berries reddened, for the chickadee that stayed.

We are shepherds still, and sore afraid.

Help us to hear, help us to believe, help us to join the angel chant:

"Glory to God in the highest, and on earth peace, good will toward men."

All men.

AMEN

Saviour who filleth the hungry with good things, we, too, would magnify the Lord.

For gloves of wool and leathern shoes, for milk in cup and meat on plate, for fragrant fire and bright-red bitter-sweet, we are thankful to thee, who giveth all.

Abiding in the fields in the short day, or watching over our flock in the long night, we believe what the angel told other shepherds: "Fear not: for, behold, I bring you good tidings of great joy, which shall be to all people."

All people? That's good. That's us.

Glory be to thee.

AMEN

Lord of all, though born to earth a mere man-child, swaddled in the fodder of a manger and first heralded by angels to us keepers of sheep, we thank thee for another birthday of God right down here among us.

We tenants who presently have this earth of thine and every living thing that moveth in our keeping are profoundly blessed that thou didst choose as the birthplace of thy Son a stable, bedded sweetly with bright straw and warmed by the fresh breath of honest farm animals, with sore shoulders, distended udders, and gentle voices.

Make us ever better herdsmen so that all thy children may have meat with their bread.

As we follow the Star, may we scatter seeds of good will so that peace may sprout all over the place.

AMEN

Sore afraid, too, we who are wont to abide in the fields, watching our flocks, come now to kneel as in a stable.

Even a cow stable, Lord, back of an inn, just as the angel told us.

And, lo, in a manger where we were wont to put hay for the kine, we found thine only begotten Son.

Given by our Father in heaven that we other children should not perish from the earth.

Immanuel!

Prince of Peace!

In a manger!

A lowly manger. Might have been our manger. Where stood the star!

For such is the Kingdom.

AMEN

THE FARMER
GIVES THANKS

SAMUEL R. GUARD

In these fifty-six prayers, arranged chron-ologically to cover the entire year, a farmer offers thanks to God in the language of a man of the soil.

Here are prayers for the seasons and months of the year, for special days from New Year's to Christmas. Included also are general petitions for the blessing of God on the farm, on its crops and its animals, and for God's people everywhere.

For the man who lives on the farm or reflects on the quiet beauty of rural life —reading and praying these prayers will bring a better appreciation of how God blesses all men through the physical world.